RADIATION

RADIATION
BENEFITS/DANGERS

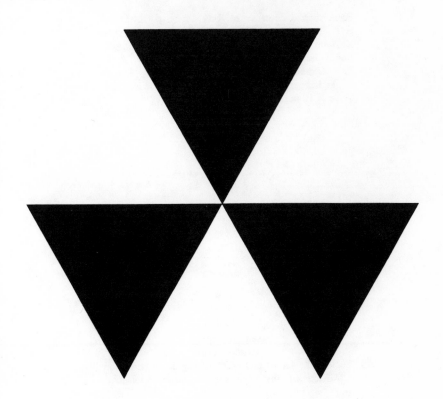

BY DINAH MOCHÉ

FRANKLIN WATTS 15935
NEW YORK / LONDON / TORONTO / 1979
AN !MPACT BOOK

Photographs courtesy of: U.S. Navy, p. 10; ERDA, p. 14; the American Cancer Society, p. 15; Argonne National Laboratory, pp. 16, 17; Brookhaven National Laboratory, pp. 24, 42; NASA, pp. 27, 36, 37; The Bettmann Archive, Inc., p. 54; Los Alamos Photo Laboratory, p. 55; the American Museum of Natural History, p. 73.

Library of Congress Cataloging in Publication Data

Moché, Dinah
Radiation: benefits/dangers.

(An Impact book)
Bibliography: p.
Includes index.
SUMMARY: Describes various forms of radiation and discusses the benefits and hazards of their use.
1. Radiation—Juvenile literature. [1. Radiation] I. Title.
QC475.25.M62   539.7′2   79–10449
ISBN 0–531–02860–7

CONTENTS

FOR REBECCA,
WHO RADIATES LOVE

RADIATION

INTRODUCTION

Everyone should know something about radiation. We are all continually bombarded by invisible rays. Some of these rays come naturally from the ground, the oceans, the air, and outer space. Other rays are released by humans in our technological society.

Powerful invisible rays can be used constructively to improve our daily lives or destructively to kill. It is not surprising that people ask many questions such as:

What is radiation?
What does it do to human bodies?
How can it be used to help us?
What are the dangers from radiation?

How much exposure is safe for people and the environment?

Are the benefits of using radiation in our daily lives worth the risks involved?

These are important questions. Experts don't agree on all the answers. Much is known, but there is more to be learned. This book gives you the latest scientific information about radiation and its effects. It describes some of the most interesting benefits controlled use of radiation brings to us and also explains why radiation can be so dangerous. It will help you think about controversial issues yourself.

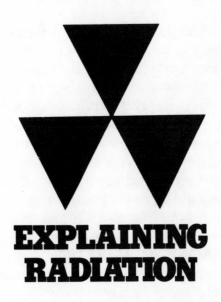

EXPLAINING RADIATION

On a warm sunny day you can see light and feel heat that were radiated into space by the sun. You can't see or feel most of the other forms of radiation that exist.

Although people have always lived with nature's radiation, scientists only recently discovered what radiation is and how to produce it.

X rays were discovered accidentally in 1895 by the German physicist Wilhelm Roentgen during his experiments on electric charges. He called the rays **X,** meaning their nature was unknown. Soon afterward, in 1896, the French physicist Antoine Henri Becquerel made another important discovery by accident. He found that the chemical element uranium spontaneously gives off rays powerful enough to leave their mark on photographic film.

Many scientists were interested in the newly discovered rays and did experiments to learn more about them. Today we know that radiation consists of energy in waves or fast-moving particles of matter. Some radiation carries enough energy to penetrate a substance and change it. Because such changes can help us or hurt us enormously, research on radiation and its effects continues to this day.

ELECTROMAGNETIC RADIATION

Light and heat are two examples of **electromagnetic radiation,** which consists of energy in waves. (Heat is also known as infrared radiation.) The waves are made up of electric and magnetic fields that can force electric charges and compasses to move. Hence, they are called **electromagnetic waves.**

Other electromagnetic waves—those that carry radio and TV shows and those used in microwave ovens and airport radar—are longer than light waves. Ultraviolet waves (which can give you a suntan), X rays (which doctors use), and gamma rays (released by deadly nuclear weapons) are shorter than light waves. But they're all basically the same kind of energy waves. They behave very differently when they hit something, because they have different wave lengths. Short waves carry more energy than long waves do.

Electromagnetic radiation comes from accelerating electric charges. It zooms through empty space at the same speed as light, 299,739 km (186,282 miles) per second. For example, accelerating electric charges in the sun send out energy in waves. Light and heat waves of energy zoom through space to hit you on earth. They force electric charges in your eyes and skin to move. Then you see and feel sunshine!

Most objects in the universe are made of **atoms.** Atoms have electric charges in their core, or **nucleus,** and orbiting the nucleus. Whenever atoms are bounced around, their electric charges accelerate and send out energy waves. So objects such as our sun and the planet Earth—and you—all radiate electromagnetic waves. The length of those waves as well as the way they behave depend on the motion of the electric charges inside.

Electromagnetic waves that carry signals to your AM radio are about 300 m (1,000 feet) long. Light waves, which you can see, are only between 40 and 70 millionths of a cm (16 and 28 millionths of an inch) long. The shortest gamma waves known are much shorter than that!

Beams of very short gamma rays and X rays carry tremendous energy. Gamma rays are shot out of an atomic nucleus when it breaks up. X rays are generated naturally in atoms by **electrons** when they change orbits or artificially in X-ray machines, where electrons are forced to strike a metal target. These high-energy, short electromagnetic waves are especially effective in producing physical, chemical, and biological changes in matter.

Scientists don't agree yet about how effectively the long electromagnetic waves change living things. Soviet scientists reported that people exposed to microwave levels lower than that considered safe by, say, the United States government (10/1,000 of a watt), felt unusually tired, had trouble thinking and remembering, and suffered pains such as headaches. In 1978, the General Accounting Office, the investigative agency of Congress, said it is possible that the public is being exposed to dangerous levels of microwave radiation. There is continuing research to find out how microwaves affect animals and to help set safe radiation levels for people.

RADIOACTIVITY

An atom whose nucleus breaks up spontaneously and emits radiation is called **radioactive.** Some materials are naturally radioactive, but many things can be made radioactive. Most radioactive materials emit three different types of radiation. They are called **alpha, beta,** and **gamma** rays, after the first three letters of the Greek alphabet.

Alpha rays are nuclei of the chemical element helium and are thus positively charged. They are heavy, but usually so weak that they can be stopped by a piece of paper. **Beta rays** are composed of electrons, which are negatively charged particles. They are much smaller and lighter than alpha particles and usually more penetrating. They can be stopped by thin pieces of wood. **Gamma rays** are very short wave (energetic) electromagnetic radiation. Powerful gamma rays can even go into concrete.

Ninety-two different chemical elements are found naturally on earth. Each one has its own atom containing a unique nucleus. Each nucleus has a specific number of positively charged particles called **protons,** from 1 (hydrogen) to 92 (uranium). For each proton in an atom, there is a negatively charged electron circling the nucleus at some distance. Chemical activity depends on the number of electrons, or protons, an atom has. Chemists list natural elements in an arrangement called the **periodic table** in order of the number of protons the elements have, from 1 to 92. Each additional proton means a new chemical element.

Every atom except (normally) the simplest, hydrogen, has electrically neutral particles called **neutrons** in the nucleus, too. Significantly, different atoms of the same chemical element can have different numbers of neutrons inside. Atoms of the same chemical element that have a different number of neutrons are called **isotopes.**

Some isotopes have a number of neutrons and protons that is "comfortable," and they are stable. Others, such as radium, have excess numbers of neutrons or protons, and they are not stable; they undergo sudden spontaneous changes to "comfortable" arrangements. During this rearrangement, the isotopes give off radiation, so they are called **radioisotopes.**

The simplest element, hydrogen, has three isotopes. All three forms of hydrogen have one proton and one electron. Over 99 percent of all hydrogen found in nature has just a proton in its nucleus. Heavy hydrogen, or deuterium, has a proton plus a neutron. Very heavy hydrogen, or tritium, has a proton plus two neutrons. Tritium is a radioisotope.

Although the isotopes of hydrogen have special names, those of other elements don't. To distinguish among the isotopes of a chemical element, we place after the element's name a number telling the combined total of protons and neutrons the isotope has. For example, a useful isotope of the element carbon has six protons and eight neutrons. It is named carbon 14.

HALF-LIFE

Radioactive materials become less active as time goes by because radioisotopes change into a form that lasts. Scientists can't predict exactly when a single atom will break up, but they can measure the time it takes for the breakup of half of the atoms in a sample of some specific radioisotope. This time is called the radioisotope's **half-life.**

Half-lives of different isotopes vary from a fraction of a second to billions of years. Materials with extremely short half-lives lose most of their radioactivity very quickly. Materials with extremely long half-lives keep sending out radiation for ages.

Radiation from radioisotopes is used in different ways to benefit humans. Each application determines what kind of radioisotope and half-life are most suitable. For detecting problems inside the human body, radioisotopes with short half-lives are usually best so that the radioactivity will disappear fast after the work is done. For power or heat sources in inaccessible places such as outer space or the ocean depths, radioisotopes with long half-lives are needed so that they won't have to be replaced frequently.

HOW RADIATION
AFFECTS MATERIALS

Gamma rays, X rays and alpha particles, electrons, and neutrons moving thousands of miles a second carry energy.

When they pass through matter, they can transfer some energy to the atoms there. Electrons in the material can be knocked out of position or even freed from the atoms. An atom that loses one or more electrons is called an **ion.** The radiation that forms ions is called **ionizing radiation.**

By knocking many electrons out of their normal position in a material, ionizing radiation can change physical characteristics of the material such as strength or hue; chemical characteristics, forming new compounds; or biological functioning such as normal growth. Its ability to cause ionization makes radiation extremely useful but also potentially harmful to humans.

Electrons freed by radiation can be collected to make radiation detecting equipment such as **Geiger counters.**

RADIOISOTOPE PRODUCTION

Most supplies of useful radioisotopes are produced regularly by neutron capture in nuclear reactors. Beams of neutrons are shot at billions of stable target atoms. A neutron is a good bullet. It has no electric charge. It easily approaches and enters a positively charged target nucleus. Then the target nucleus has more than its normal, "comfortable," amount of particles and energy. It has been made into a radioisotope!

For example, the element cobalt normally has 27 protons and 32 neutrons. When a rod of cobalt is bombarded by neutrons in a nuclear reactor, a few cobalt atoms capture one neutron and then have 33 neutrons. They have been changed from cobalt 59, which is found commonly in nature, to cobalt 60. Cobalt 60 is a radioisotope. It gives off gamma and beta rays. Cobalt 60 has a half-life of 5.26 years and is useful for treating cancer patients.

[9]

A laboratory technician uses a Geiger counter
to measure the radioactivity in this rabbit's blood.

When the heaviest natural element, uranium, is bombarded with neutrons, it can capture a neutron, have nuclear changes, and be left with 93 protons. It is changed to neptunium, an element not found in nature. Further nuclear changes form an element with 94 protons, called plutonium. So far, scientists have produced 14 elements that are not found in nature, from neptunium, with 93 protons, to an element with 106 protons that is not yet officially named.

A neutron fired at the proper speed at a heavy atom such as uranium can enter the target nucleus and cause fission. **Atomic fission** is the splitting of a nucleus into chunks that are radioisotopes. During fission, large amounts of energy are released. Fission energy is harnessed in nuclear power plants to generate electrical power. It is also the power source of the atomic bomb.

TRACERS

Radiation lets us "see" things that we can't look at normally. Powerful gamma and beta rays burst through walls that stop light. Radiation detection equipment can uncode the information they bring.

To follow something we can't watch directly, such as blood circulating inside the body or oil flowing through a buried pipeline, scientists put radioisotopes into the system. Radioisotopes behave chemically exactly like normal atoms of the same kind. But they can be detected by the radiations they shoot out. These radiations help reveal what is going on. Radioisotopes used in this way are nicknamed **tracers.** Tracers are widely used in medicine, science, agriculture, and industry.

DIAGNOSING HEALTH PROBLEMS

Doctors use radioisotopes that concentrate in specific parts of the body and have safe radiation half-life, type, and energy. Iodine 131 is used in locating problems in the thyroid gland; sodium 24, in blood circulation; and phosphorus 32, in the eyeball.

For example, our thyroid gland, located at the base of the neck, controls the way in which our body converts food to energy. Iodine tends to concentrate there. A doctor gives a person suspected of having thyroid trouble a drink containing a tiny amount of iodine 131. It goes to the thyroid gland. Gamma rays shot out by the iodine 131 are detected outside the body with a radiation detector. An abnormally large number of gamma rays may indicate trouble, since an unhealthy thyroid gland takes up more iodine than a healthy one does.

The doctor can even get a picture of the thyroid gland from the radiation. An instrument called a **scanner** sweeps outside the body in a regular pattern over the whole problem area, measuring gamma rays. The result can be displayed as a visible image of the thyroid gland. Today, doctors can use scanning equipment and appropriate radioisotopes to help diagnose other problems in body areas such as the brain, liver, and lungs without having to operate.

For example, the U.S. Department of Energy announced a new way for doctors to diagnose lung diseases that make breathing difficult. Patients breathe in air containing a small amount of radioactive krypton gas. As each krypton atom decays, it shoots out a gamma ray that can be detected on a television-like video display tube. When the patient's lungs are filled with the krypton-air mixture, thou-

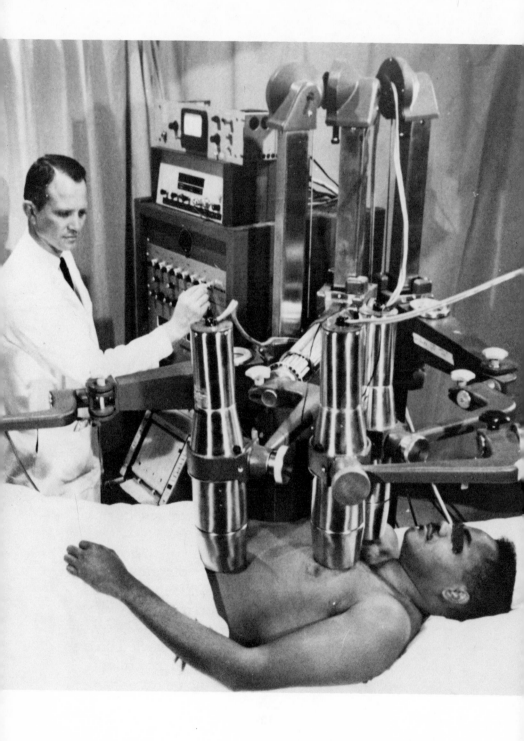

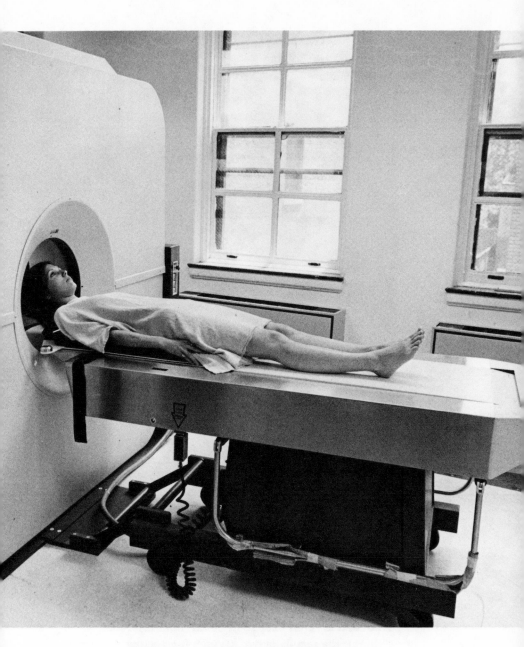

**Two kinds of modern diagnostic scanners,
both making use of radioisotopes.**

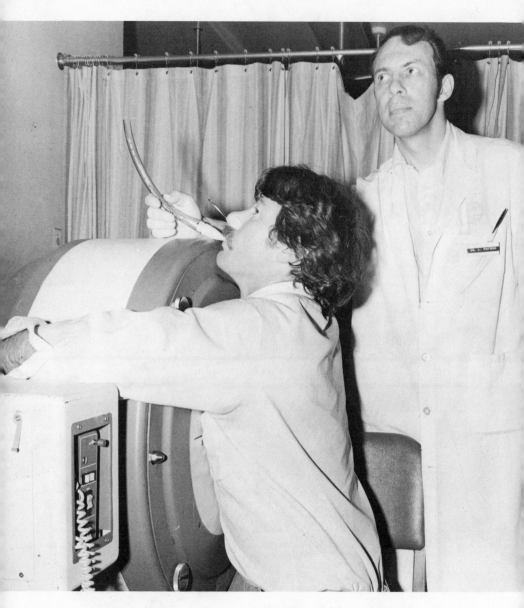

Above: a krypton lung scan being administered.
Right: the results of two krypton lung scans.
The one on top is from a patient with emphysema.
The one below is from a patient with healthy lungs.

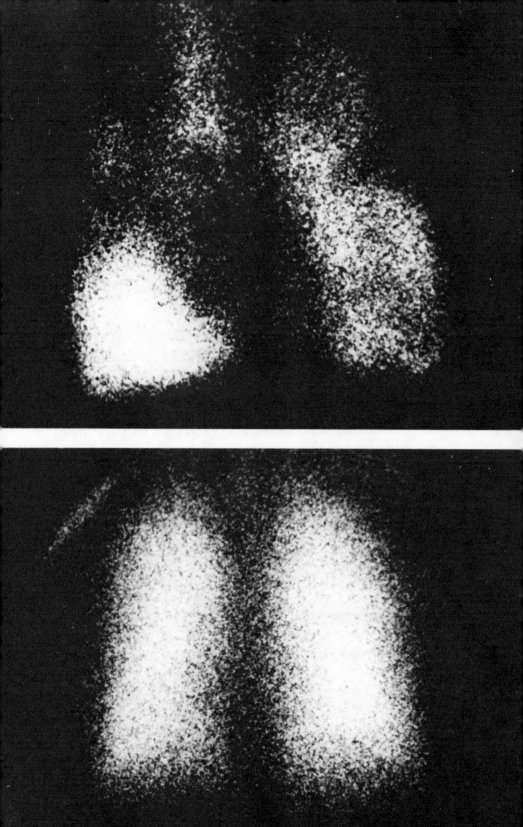

sands of flashes on the video tube create a picture of the lungs. Areas where the lungs are blocked show immediately as holes or dark spots.

Less than 20 minutes are needed to record images of a patient's lungs from the front, rear, and both sides while the person sits or lies quietly and breathes normally. The patient's total radiation exposure is less than half that received from a normal chest X ray. No radioactive gas is kept in the lungs. The test is painless and doctors think it's safe.

PLANT LIFE

Radioactive carbon 14 is an excellent tracer for studying plant life. All plants (and animals) have molecules that contain carbon atoms. In a process called **photosynthesis,** living plants take in carbon dioxide and water and change them into sugar, using the energy of sunlight.

Scientists have used carbon 14 to find out just exactly how photosynthesis works. American biochemist Melvin Calvin received the 1961 Nobel Prize in chemistry for identifying chemical steps that lead from carbon dioxide to sugar by using carbon 14 as a tracer.

Phosphorus 32 has helped farmers use fertilizer more effectively. Radioactive phosphorus 32 is mixed into ordinary fertilizers. When plants take up the fertilizer, radiation from the leaves is measured. Scientists then figure out when, where, and how to put fertilizer for best results.

For example, they have found that most fertilizer is used in the first two or three weeks. It can be absorbed through leaves and bark much more effectively than from the ground. Now fertilizer is added to insect sprays.

IS THERE LIFE ON MARS?

Scientists on Earth used radioactive carbon 14 to help them look for life processes on Mars, 320 million km (200 million miles) away. Two robot spacecraft named Viking did the tests in 1976 and 1977.

Each Viking robot carried an automated laboratory the size of a typewriter. The tiny laboratories were operated by remote control from Earth. They could do the work of three complete biological laboratories with technicians, and radio their findings back to Earth. The robots did several tests for signs of life in the Martian soil.

One test was designed to look for living microbes. A pinch of soil was taken and loaded into a test cell. It was moistened with a nutrient nicknamed "chicken soup" containing some carbon 14 atoms. If microbes lived in the soil, presumably they would eat the food, digest it, and use it to grow and reproduce. Some radioactive carbon dioxide would be given off as a waste product. A radiation detector was set nearby to signal the arrival of radioactive carbon dioxide, which would suggest that microbes lived in the soil.

When the test was performed, the radiation detector indicated that a lot of radioactive carbon dioxide had been produced.

Another test looked for photosynthesis in living plants. A pinch of soil was put into a container and exposed to artificial Martian air made of mostly carbon dioxide gas with some radioactive carbon 14 and water vapor. The sample was bathed in artificial Martian sunlight. If Martian plants lived in the soil, presumably they would take in carbon dioxide and water and change them to sugar as they grew. After five days the soil was tested to see if it contained carbon 14, which would suggest plants lived there.

When the test was performed, the soil was found to be radioactive.

Scientists do not agree about what the tests for life on Mars mean. The experiments showed activity in the soil. It might be due to living microbes. But the results could also be explained by complicated chemical reactions. Different tests suggested that no familiar microbes exist on Mars.

The test results remain puzzling. Scientists are continuing tests in laboratories here. They hope to send new robots to do more tests on Mars to find out if any Martian microbes live there.

CAR MANUFACTURING

A good place to see how industry uses tracers is in car manufacturing. Engineers find out how parts of an automobile engine such as piston rings wear during use by making them radioactive. The engine is run, and the piston rings rub against the walls. A small amount of radioactive iron 59 wears off and falls into the lubricating oil. The oil is pumped past a radiation detector. The amount of radiation detected indicates the rate of wear. Using different oils, engineers can find the one that gives the longest life to the engine.

Tires can be made more efficient in a similar way. Radioactive phosphorus 32 is put in the tread of tires. Then they are mounted on a car, and the car is driven. Radiations from the phosphorus 32 are measured by a detector set under the car's bumper. Tire wear is figured out from the decrease in the amount of radiation detected. Studies of how tire wear depends on factors such as the car's speed and load, and road conditions, have been done.

PIPELINES

Tracers are very helpful for finding holes or blocks in all kinds of pipes. They save a lot of digging if the pipe is buried underground!

For example, oil and natural gas are commonly shipped long distances through pipelines. Sometimes leaks develop. Sometimes objects block the flow in the pipes. Leaks and blocks in pipelines are located by putting a radioactive substance into the fluid they carry and measuring the radiations it sends out along the pipe.

Different oil companies often use the same pipeline. All oil looks alike. But oil belonging to different companies can be "branded" like cattle belonging to different ranches by putting a very small amount of radioisotope at the front of each batch. The oil flows a long distance from the source to storage tanks. When it gets to the place where the tanks are, radiation detectors monitor the radioisotopes. Then each company's oil is routed to its own tanks.

DATING GAMES

Radiation emitted from ancient objects provides important clues as to their ages. Scientists take a small sample of an object. Then they measure the radiation shot out by radioisotopes of known half-life.

Half of a group of radioisotopes, or "parent" atoms, changes into atoms of a different kind, or "daughter" atoms, in one half-life. The older a sample is, the fewer parents and the more daughters it has, and the less radiation it emits. From the radiation detected, scientists can compare the ratio of parents to daughters. Then they figure out the object's age.

RADIOCARBON DATING

Archaeologists study the life and culture of ancient peoples. They learn about our early ancestors by digging up things that were left behind. Skeletons, tools, clothing, and scrolls reveal a lot.

A basic question about these things is how old they are. If they contain carbon originally taken from Earth's atmosphere, scientists can get the answer by the method of radiocarbon (carbon 14) dating.

Our atmosphere contains normal carbon 12 atoms plus some radioactive carbon 14 atoms. Both of these carbon isotopes act the same chemically. Both occur mainly in carbon dioxide gas (carbon combined with oxygen). Plants use this carbon dioxide in photosynthesis. Animals eat plants or plant-eating animals. So all living plants and animals have some carbon 14 in them.

Living things have the same ratio of carbon 14 to carbon 12 as the atmosphere has. After death, this ratio goes down. The half-life of carbon 14 is 5,730 years. The carbon 14 atoms present keep changing to nitrogen 14, and no new carbon 14 is taken in.

By determining the present ratio of carbon 14 to carbon 12 in a sample from something that lived up to 40,000 years ago, scientists can figure out its age.

Imagine that in a leather garment found in a tribal burial site, the ratio of carbon 14 to carbon 12 is one-half that in our atmosphere. How old is it? You figure the leather must date from an animal that died one half-life, or 5,730 years, ago.

Two prehistoric skeletons wrapped in burial garments, now displayed in the Buffalo Bill Museum

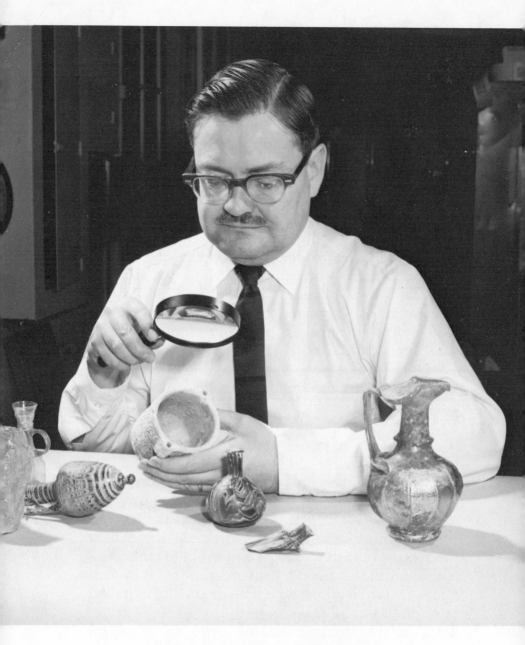

A chemist studies the composition of these
artifacts in order to date them properly.

in Cody, Wyoming, were dated in just this way. They had roamed Wyoming in the eighth century B.C.! Tools and animal bones which have been radiocarbon dated suggest that people first lived in the western United States 16,000 years ago.

Some astounding giant bear bones turned up in a sand and gravel pit in Kearns, Utah, in 1978. Paleontologist James H. Madsen, Jr., having samples checked by radiocarbon dating, estimated that the Pleistocene bear lived about 18,000 years ago. Apparently this huge prehistoric animal stood over 3½ m (nearly 12 feet) upright, about 1 m (3 feet) taller than polar bears and 1.5 m (5 feet) taller than average grizzly bears today.

HOW OLD IS THE PLANET EARTH?

Geologists calculate the age of rocks using radioisotopes whose half-lives are many millions of years. Their estimates are based on the ratio of parent to daughter atoms present in a rock. This assumes that since the rock was formed, the parent content has been changed only by radioactive decay and no daughter products have been lost.

Uranium 238 changes to lead 206 with a half-life of 4,500,000,000 years, and uranium 235 changes to lead 207 with a half-life of 710,000,000 years. A rock that has uranium also has some of these uncommon lead isotopes. For some very old rocks, the ratio of uranium 238 to lead 206 has yielded ages of approximately 3,000,000,000 years.

Many rocks contain the element rubidium. Rubidium 87 has a half-life of 50,000,000,000 years. It changes to strontium 87. The ratio of parent rubidium 87 to daughter strontium 87 reveals the rock's age.

The oldest rocks found in the United States so far are in Wyoming and Minnesota. They are over 3,000,000,000 years old. In the United Kingdom the oldest rocks are in northwest Scotland and are approximately 2,700,000,000 years old. The oldest rocks known anywhere in the world are in Greenland. These are over 3,600,000,000 years old.

Our planet must be even older than the oldest rocks discovered. Rocks that were on the surface when Earth was born must have disappeared long ago. Earth's surface is constantly changed by the forces of erosion, volcanism, and drifting continents.

Current theory says that Earth formed together with all the other bodies in our solar system from a single huge swirling cloud of gas and dust. Meteorites are primitive chunks of stone or metal from our solar system that land on Earth. Presumably they were formed when Earth was, and have not been changed since.

Radioactive dating of meteorites suggests that they are some 4,600,000,000 years old. Geologists, using data from the radioactive decay of uranium in rocks and other geological information, figure that the earth is also about 4,600,000,000 years old.

MOON ROCKS

Six Apollo moon missions between 1969 and 1972 landed 12 astronauts on the moon. They brought back 382 kg (843 pounds) of moon rock and soil for laboratory analysis. Three unmanned Soviet Luna spacecraft have returned several ounces more. This material is still being studied by scientists today.

The moon rocks were dated using rubidium-strontium dating and other methods. The youngest are 3,100,000,000 to 3,800,000,000 years old.

It is hoped that the Apollo 15 moon rocks
will eventually tell us how old our Earth is.

Many samples from the moon's highlands are from 4,000,000,000 to 4,300,000,000 years old.

A few moon rocks provide evidence that the moon was formed at the same time as Earth and meteorites. Tiny green rock fragments collected by the last Apollo (17) astronauts are some 4,600,000,000 years old! Another Apollo 17 crystalline rock was assigned the same age in 1976. These fragments could be some of the first material that solidified on the moon.

RADIOISOTOPE DATING WITH ACCELERATORS

A promising new technique for dating objects was proposed by the physicist Richard A. Muller in 1977. It is more sensitive than the standard method of measuring radiation from radioisotopes. It can measure much smaller and older samples than was ever before possible.

Minute samples of the material being examined are turned into a gas. The gas is accelerated to velocities greater than a thousand miles per second by giant accelerators (atom-smashing machines) such as cyclotrons. Speeding individual atoms penetrate thin silicon detectors. They cause a short electrical pulse to flow which identifies them. Radioactive atoms can be detected with great sensitivity. One atom in 1,000,000,000,000 can be found in just a few minutes!

This technique will be especially useful for determining the age of very precious, irreplaceable old objects. Only remarkably small samples are needed. It needs only a chip of the object that is up to a thousand times smaller than that required by the standard method. Tiny bits of wood, rock, and bone have already been tested successfully.

Some intriguing carbon-bearing objects are so old that most of their carbon 14 is gone. Whatever radiation comes out is simply undetectable, making standard radiocarbon dating impossible. Muller expects to be able to date such objects that lived up to 100,000 years ago quite accurately with the new technique.

It will also be possible to determine the ages of rocks and sediments that have been in the earth for as long as 30 million years. Beryllium 10 can be detected in small samples of rock. Detected in marine deposits, it has been used to study the ocean bottom.

Beryllium 10 can now be used to develop a dating system for sedimentary rocks. It likely will become a tool as powerful for geology as radiocarbon dating has been for archaeology. It can tell geologists many things about the earth.

INSIDE VIEW

Radiography is a process of taking pictures with radiation other than normal light. X-ray pictures taken by a doctor or dentist are familiar examples. Most radiographs are made with X rays and gamma rays.

These radiations are more energetic than ordinary light. They easily shoot through objects that stop light rays. The amount of radiation that gets through depends on the density and thickness of the material inside. This is the basis for taking pictures of hidden things like bones inside the body or guns inside locked suitcases.

X rays and gamma rays have been detected coming from outer space. Their energies are so great that they have not yet been reproduced in the largest accelerators on Earth. These high energy radiations give clues about the structure, composition, and energy processes deep inside the stars and galaxies that produce them. High energy astronomy is an exciting new way to probe mysterious secrets of the universe.

MEDICAL AND DENTAL X RAYS

You may have had medical or dental X rays and wondered how they work. A part of your body is placed in front of a beam of X rays. Some of the X rays get through while others are absorbed or scattered inside your body. When the X rays strike photographic film or a display screen, shadows of the denser parts of the body appear. Differences in the X-ray shadows cast by bones, tissues, fluids, and air in the body tell a doctor's trained eye a lot.

For example, when a skater breaks a leg in an ice hockey game, the doctor has to know the exact position and nature of the fracture to set it properly. An X-ray picture of the broken leg will do the trick.

The skater's leg is placed against a panel that holds X-ray film. X rays come from an X-ray machine through the broken leg and expose the film. Medical and dental diagnostic X rays can pass through about 10 cm (4 inches) of fleshy material but are absorbed by most bony structures. The skater's film is exposed (looks dark) in the areas corresponding to the fleshy material but not in the areas blocked by bone (where the film looks light). Thus X rays show the nature of the fracture.

Dentists take X-ray pictures of teeth the same way. X rays from an X-ray machine are directed toward the teeth and a small piece of film. Teeth, fillings, gums, and jawbone all absorb different amounts of X rays from the beam. Problems inside the teeth show up in the resulting picture on the film when it is developed.

Sometimes patients must swallow a substance called a **contrast medium** before an X-ray picture is taken. The first contrast medium was just air. During a chest X ray, patients hold a deep breath to keep their lungs filled with air. X rays zip through air so easily that lung tissues show up on the film. Cloudy spots on the film show trouble areas.

For gastrointestinal, or GI, X-ray pictures, the contrast medium could be barium. Barium is a **radiopaque material** (absorbs X rays). It helps doctors spot trouble in the esophagus, stomach, and intestines. Children who have swallowed a sharp pin or bone know these pictures help the doctor retrieve it from their gastrointestinal tracts.

A **fluoroscope** is a device that displays X-ray shadow pictures directly. X rays are sent through a patient to strike a fluorescent screen that gives off visible light when they hit. Doctors can thus watch materials such as barium flow through body organs like the stomach.

Visualization of the blood vessels is called **angiography.** A radiologist is a doctor specially trained to use X rays and other radiations in medicine. Radiologists insert a catheter, or plastic tube, into a vein or artery. Then they inject a contrast medium that can be seen in an X-ray picture. Angiography has been useful in diagnosing heart and brain problems.

The ability of X rays to penetrate our bodies, which makes them useful for medical diagnosis, also makes them potentially harmful. Excessive doses of X rays can be deadly. X-ray pictures should be taken only when there is an absolutely necessary medical reason. The section titled **Effects on People** details the dangers involved.

MAKING X RAYS SAFER

New methods are aimed at decreasing the X-ray dose patients get when they need X-ray pictures. The length of time patients are required to be exposed to X rays is being shortened. The amount of radiation used is being lowered.

New high-speed X-ray films reduce the time of exposure necessary for a typical X-ray picture. Older fluoroscopes exposed patients to more X rays than films would. Modern fluoroscopes have electronic image intensifiers that give good pictures with reduced exposure. Some also have foot pedals to turn the X rays on and off and film to record important pictures that doctors can study freely afterward.

X-ray researcher Lo I Yin produced instant X-ray pictures with a small source of radioactive material in 1977. His new device is called a **lixiscope,** for **low** in**tensity X-ray i**maging **scope.**

The lixiscope converts a very low dose of X rays to a visible picture on the spot using high image intensification. It is held in one hand. Easy to carry around, the lixiscope should be useful wherever a quick X-ray picture is desirable. Potential emergency examinations range from determining a football player's possible bone injury on the field to discovering a gas leak in a pipe.

SECURITY CHECKS

You see X-ray fluoroscope scanning systems at many airports and in public buildings. The threat of

violence is so great in the world that all closed suitcases and packages are suspect. Public security
calls for a look inside.

Government concern about aircraft highjacking
and bomb threats became so great that federal regulations today require inspection of all passengers
and baggage before they board commercial aircraft. Passengers walk next to a conveyor belt that
takes baggage past an X-ray fluoroscope unit that
looks for hidden weapons or explosives. Radiation
output from these machines is kept extremely low to
protect passengers. Your photographic film could go
through the machine about five times and still be
used.

X-ray units were sometimes used in shipyards
and factories during World War II to inspect people
for security reasons. Personnel inspection by X rays
was cut out because X rays can be so deadly. Today
terrorists threaten world peace, and some personnel
X-ray scanning systems to detect metallic objects
are being used again. Modern systems are designed
to give much smaller X-ray doses than older ones.

GAMMA RAY PICTURES

Gamma rays are similar to X rays and even more
penetrating. They are also used to make pictures.
Portable gamma ray sources (radioisotopes) are
smaller and easier to move than typical X-ray machines. So gamma rays are used especially for taking pictures in places that are hard to get to.

Radioisotopes are put inside complicated ma-
chinery. Gamma rays give "inside-out" views that
X-ray machines can't. Gamma rays from cobalt 60
detect flaws inside rail wheels and car engines.

Those from gadolinium 153 make inside-out pictures of aluminum pistons at automotive research laboratories. Others inspect aircraft parts for small cracks that might grow and lead to failure in flight.

HIGH ENERGY ASTRONOMY

Powerful, deadly X rays and gamma rays pour down on Earth from outer space. Fortunately for humans, they are absorbed by our atmosphere before they can strike us. These radiations bring important information about mysterious space objects that produce them.

High energy astronomy is a new field. Astronomers send their instruments above our atmosphere. They study the X rays, gamma rays, and **cosmic rays** (extremely energetic atomic nuclei and electrons) originating in outer space. These high energy radiations give clues about intriguing objects such as quasars, pulsars, and black holes that still baffle astronomers.

Quasars, short for "quasi-stellar radio sources," look like stars when viewed through an optical telescope but emit more energy in radio waves than the most powerful galaxies known. If they are as distant as many astronomers think, the total amount of energy emitted by a quasar in one second would supply all of Earth's electrical energy needs for 1,000,000,000 years!

Pulsars, discovered in 1967, flash radio signals regularly. They seem to be rapidly rotating stars. They are likely made of densely packed neutrons formed when a massive star dies.

Black holes are thought to be the final stage in the collapse of a dying massive star. Matter is

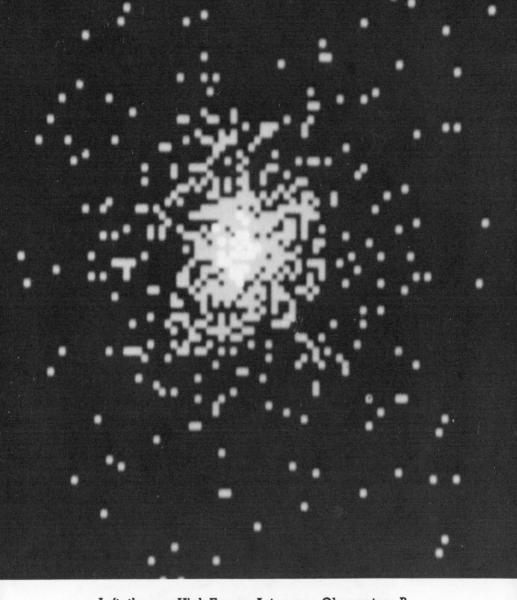

Left: the new High Energy Astronomy Observatory-B
before launch, expected by scientists to help us
unlock many of the secrets of the universe. Above:
the very first picture of an X-ray star, transmitted
from NASA's new High Energy Astronomy Observatory
on November 18, 1978. The star is Cygnus X-1,
part of a star system thought to contain a black hole.

packed extraordinarily densely in a black hole. The force of gravity is so great that nothing, not even light, can escape from a black hole.

Physicists Riccardo Giacconi and Herbert Friedman founded X-ray astronomy in 1962. The X-ray sources identified in space since then are the most energetic objects seen in the universe. Progress in gamma ray astronomy has been slower because sources are weaker and detectors are less efficient. Short, intense bursts of gamma rays have been detected from various parts of the sky. No one knows where they come from yet, although interesting guesses have been made.

High Energy Astronomy Observatories (HEAO), robot spacecraft launched by the U.S. National Aeronautics and Space Administration (NASA) between 1977 and 1979, orbited Earth at an altitude of about 412 km (256 miles). Their scientific instruments detected X rays, gamma rays, and cosmic rays from outer space. Astronomers are analyzing the data and hope they will learn how the extremely high energies are generated. Expect new facts about the amazing quasars, pulsars, and black holes in the next few years.

POSITIVE
IDENTIFICATION

Crime investigators looking for a trace of poison in a murder victim, art dealers trying to decide if a painting is a forgery, and doctors trying to find minute traces of enzymes in the body all turn to radiation.

Radiation can positively identify a chemical element in a sample of material even where the amount is amazingly small.

NEUTRON ACTIVATION ANALYSIS
One efficient method of detecting a trace of a chemical element in an object is to bombard a sample with neutrons. Stable atoms are changed into radioactive ones. They spit out gamma rays that are observed with radiation detectors.

[39]

At least 70 of the chemical elements can be activated by neutron bombardment. Each kind of radioisotope changes to a stable form in a unique way. Each has a characteristic half-life and radiation type and energy. These are listed in scientific reference books.

Scientists analyze the gamma rays they detect. They compare this radiation with the characteristics of different radioisotopes. Then they can tell which unique decay pattern is revealed by emitted radiations, and which elements were in the sample at the start. This method is called **neutron activation analysis.**

LAW ENFORCEMENT

Neutron activation analysis is used to help solve crimes. Human hair identifies a person just as fingerprints do. Hair contains small amounts of metallic elements such as gold and copper. The amounts are about the same in all the hairs on an individual's head but vary considerably from person to person.

Hair left at the scene of a crime can be bombarded by neutrons. The resulting radiation is analyzed. This "hairprint" is then compared to hairprints of suspected criminals in the case. When hairs match, it is strong evidence the suspect was at the site.

Many historians long suspected that French Emperor Napoleon I (1769–1821) did not die a natural death. Samples of Napoleon Bonaparte's hair were sent for neutron activation analysis. Scientists found much more arsenic in his hair than is normal for healthy people. Apparently Napoleon was slowly poisoned to death on the island of St. Helena!

When a murder victim has been shot, neutron

activation analysis of the wipings from a suspect's hand can be used to find the killer. Gunpowder leaves minute amounts of metals such as antimony, barium, and copper on a killer's hand. If traces of these elements in the wipings are found to match those on the murder gun, the suspect likely fired the gun.

Hit-and-run cars can be identified this way, too. Cars usually lose some paint or grease in an accident. Specks of paint or grease from a suspected car are analyzed to see if they match the bits of material left behind at the accident site.

FAKES AND FORGERIES

Artistic masterpieces are very valuable. Paintings by famous artists and rare old artifacts command high prices from collectors. Of course, fakes and forgeries are worthless even if they look just like the real thing. Scientists use neutron activation analysis to decide questions of authenticity in art and archaeology.

Paints have changed through the years. The fractional concentration of impurities in the lead pigments used in oil paintings today is not the same as in paints used hundreds of years ago. Technological advances have changed the way lead is refined. Lead refined before 1650 is recognized by traces of chromium, which don't appear later. Lead refined after 1950 is recognizable by traces of zinc and antimony, which don't appear earlier.

Information about lead impurities reveals the era in which an oil painting was done.

Imagine that someone claims to have found a previously unknown early painting by the Dutch artist Rembrandt van Rijn (1606–1669). If analysis

Various autoradiograph tests revealed the
authenticity of this painting by Marian Blakelock.

shows the lead pigment contains traces of zinc and antimony, can the painting be an early Rembrandt? It could hardly have been done by the great master if the paint is modern and unlike any that he used!

Physicist Maurice Cotter and chemist Kathleen Taylor bombarded whole oil paintings with neutrons. Some were by the American artist Ralph A. Blakelock (1847–1919). The paintings became slightly radioactive, but only temporarily. They were ready to be rehung in a museum only two months later.

The gamma rays that shot out were analyzed to find out which radioisotopes were present in the painting. Beta rays shot out, too. They were captured on film next to the painting, making pictures called autoradiographs when they hit.

An autoradiograph reveals layers of different materials under a finished painting. Autoradiographs can be used together with X-ray pictures to see the stages of an artist's work, underpaintings that were later painted over, parts of a painting done by students, and forgeries. They are useful in art history and conservation, as well as in detecting fakes.

POLLUTION
Pollution is one of the most important problems humans face today. Our technological society produces millions of tons of wastes. It can be difficult and costly to dispose of these wastes without polluting the environment. Sometimes hazardous pollutants are released into the air or dumped into the water or ground by people who think more about saving money than about saving the environment.

The U.S. Environmental Protection Agency

(EPA) today faces many controversial questions such as how strict emission standards should be for new power plants and how many coastal cities should be allowed to discharge raw sewage into the ocean. Concerned people monitor air, water, and land for pollutants that are injurious to health. Researchers utilize neutron activation analysis to find traces of irritating elements.

For example, they examine dust falling on a city. When they find dangerous pollutants, they can track down the source. Then authorities can act to lower the amount of pollutant in the air and try to prevent further violations of legal clean air standards.

RADIOIMMUNOASSAY

A new technique for finding traces of substances in the body, **radioimmunoassay,** is so sensitive that it can measure hormones in amounts as small as 1/1,000,000,000 of a gram (4/100,000,000,000 of an ounce). A hormone is a body chemical produced by some organ and carried by the blood to other parts of the body. Hormones regulate growth and action of body organs. Her role in developing this important assay (test) won a Nobel Prize in the category of physiology or medicine in 1977 for physicist Rosalyn S. Yalow.

Radioimmunoassay combines radiation and chemical analysis. Happily, it is done in a test tube so no radiation is introduced into a patient's body. The technique involves combining a hormone with its antibody. Then a small amount of a radioactive form of the hormone is introduced. The radioactive and nonradioactive hormones compete with each other for the antibody. From measurements of how

[44]

much of the radioactive form survives the competition, scientists can figure out the original hormone concentration in the body.

Doctors are using radioimmunoassay to diagnose many otherwise undetectable conditions. It can measure the concentrations of enzymes, drugs, and virtually anything else in body fluids and tissues.

Radioimmunoassay is very useful in criminal investigations, too. When there is a case of suspected poisoning, toxicologists test tissue samples from the liver or kidney of the alleged victim. Detection of traces of poisons there is a powerful source of evidence of murder.

NEAR AND FAR

Modern technology utilizes radiation in many ways besides those already discussed. Radiation helps in the manufacture of many familiar consumer products. Far out in space, it powers robot explorers.

MEASUREMENT AND CONTROL
Quality control is important in manufacturing. Items that are made on a mass production basis must come out identical. All sheets of paper in a batch must be the same size, and all similar vitamin capsules must be filled to the same level.

Radiation gauges can be used to ensure that all items on a production line meet exact thickness, level, or density specifications. In many modern industries, they measure products accurately to within a few hundred-thousandths of an inch (about the diameter of a human hair). They can provide accuracy to within a millionth of an inch if necessary. (An inch equals 2.54 cm.)

A typical production line gauge consists of a box containing a radioisotope that emits alpha, beta, or gamma rays, a radiation detector, and an indicator. The item being measured moves between the radiation source and the detector. Radiation shoots through the item to the detector. The amount of radiation that reaches the detector reveals whether the item meets the required specifications. Measurements can be automatically recorded or used immediately to adjust production.

For example, in a paper manufacturing plant, a thickness gauge is useful. A beta ray source such as krypton 85 or strontium 90 is on one side of the paper sheets and a radiation detector is on the other as the paper sheets are rolled out rapidly by machines. The amount of radiation that gets through a sheet depends on the thickness of the paper. The thickness is measured and controlled as production goes on so that all the paper coming out is uniform.

In a plant where liquids are canned, a level gauge is useful. A gamma ray source such as cobalt 60 is placed on one side of a conveyor system and a radiation detector on the opposite side. Radiation is aimed through the cans as they move by. When cans are filled to the desired level, the detector registers a specific counting rate. If the cans are not filled high enough, the counting rate jumps up above normal. If they are filled too high, the counting rate plunges below normal. A control device can be attached to reject all cans not filled correctly. In this way every accepted can that comes off the production line meets the manufacturer's standards.

RADIATION PROCESSING

When high energy radiation strikes materials, it changes them. Small molecules may be induced to combine into larger units. Large molecules may be bent or broken. Because these changes can result in better products, industry uses radiation to bring about desired chemical reactions.

The Dow Chemical Company uses gamma radiation to make a chemical called ethyl bromide. Two simple gases, ethylene and hydrogen bromide, are mixed together in a large tank, with the gamma radiation source cobalt 60 placed in the middle. Gamma rays make the two gases combine to form liquid ethyl bromide, which is then piped out. Ethyl bromide is used in the manufacture of drugs and as a fuel additive.

Plastics such as polyethylene can be improved by irradiation. Radiation causes some of the molecules to break and combine with others, a process called **cross-linking.** Cross-linking strengthens some plastics. An irradiated plastic spoon doesn't crumble in the hot water of a dishwasher as a weaker one does. Cross-linking can also be accomplished using heat, but radiation processing is often faster, cheaper, and easier to control.

Wood may be made harder by soaking it in a simple chemical and irradiating the soaked piece. The small chemical molecules combine between the fibrous tissues of the wood to make a plastic without changing the wood's beauty. The hardened product has a variety of uses that softer wood doesn't.

[48]

Textiles can be improved by radiation, too. When cotton, a very complex molecule, is joined to a simple organic chemical by irradiation, the cloth can acquire permanent-press or soil-release properties. This enormously simplifies daily clothing-care chores.

STERILIZATION

Radiation can kill living things by changing their basic molecules. Industry uses strong doses of ionizing radiation to destroy microbes. Hospital supplies such as hypodermic syringes and sutures are sterilized by irradiation. (They don't become radioactive because the low energy electrons and gamma rays used don't alter atomic nuclei.)

Surgeons use sutures to close cuts made during operations. Surgical sutures are packaged individually because they are used one at a time as needed. Each suture must be free of germs. Heat treatments can sterilize sutures, but irradiation is better because it doesn't destroy the packaging in the process of killing microbes.

Packages of sutures are put on a conveyor belt that carries them past a beam of electrons or gamma rays. They remain in the radiation beam long enough for germs to be completely destroyed. The conveyor belt brings the sterile packages out of the unit, and they are then boxed for shipping.

An important recycling effort is under way at Sandia Laboratories. Sewage sludge could be used as a conditioner on croplands or garden soil if it didn't contain poisonous germs. Sandia is constructing a pilot plant where 30- to 60-pound (approx. 13 to 26 kg) buckets of dried or composted sludge are passed over and under intense gamma radiation from cesium 137. Gamma rays kill the germs. Sandia thinks its clean sludge is safe enough to eat! Nutritionist Stan Smith is experimentally feeding it as a food supplement to cattle and sheep in New Mexico State University's Range and Animal Sciences Department.

Gamma rays have been used experimentally to kill microbes that attack food and cause it to spoil. When the microbes are destroyed, fresh meats and vegetables last much longer than usual without refrigeration. The U.S. Army has experimented with preserving selected foods by irradiation. More research is necessary before irradiation could replace other methods of preserving foods for the public. While gamma rays kill microbes, they may also chemically change the food into compounds with properties that are hazardous to human health. They sometimes cause undesirable changes in food shade, flavor, smell, and texture.

ENERGY AND POWER

Radiation energy is useful for providing power for instruments in places that are hard to reach. When energetic alpha, beta, or gamma rays are stopped in a dense material, their energy is converted to heat. Thermocouples transform small amounts of this heat to electricity.

Energy released by the radioactive decay of plutonium 238 provides power for instruments in space and at unmanned weather stations in remote areas on Earth. Three experimental packages placed on the moon by Apollo astronauts were powered by this energy. They sent data to Earth until they were turned off by NASA in 1977.

Two unmanned spacecraft named Voyager 1 and 2 were launched by NASA in the summer of 1977 to probe and radio back data about planets and their moons in the dimly lit outer part of our solar system. Their flight plan included fly-bys of Jupiter in 1979, Saturn in 1980 (Voyager 1) and 1981 (Voyager 2), and possibly Uranus in 1986.

Spacecraft that fly near Earth carry solar cells to convert sunlight to electricity for the instruments and electronics aboard. But at Jupiter, sunlight is less than 1/25 as bright as Earth's sunlight. At Uranus, some 2,870,000,000 km (1,720,000,000 miles) from the sun, it is not even 1/350 as bright. The Voyagers cannot rely on sunlight for electricity. Instead, they each have an array of three radioisotope (plutonium 238) thermoelectric generators.

The generators are on a boom extended from the spacecraft to prevent their radiation from affecting scientific instruments. Each has a maximum electrical power output of 160 watts at the beginning of the mission. The power output decreases gradually as time goes by and the radioisotopes become less active.

When the spacecraft passes Saturn, the total power available for radio communication with earth, science instruments, and spacecraft cruise needs is about 400 watts.

EFFECTS ON PEOPLE

All kinds of ionizing radiation are potentially harmful to people.

Our bodies are made of cells built of atoms. Ionizing radiation striking an individual can knock electrons out of atoms and change the makeup of cells so drastically that they can't do their normal work. This cell damage can make the individual ill immediately or at a later time (**somatic** effects) or harm future descendants (**genetic** effects).

SOMATIC EFFECTS
The changes radiation produces in body cells are not yet completely understood. Damage to the DNA

(deoxyribonucleic acid) molecule in a cell seems to be very important. DNA has the information necessary for body cells to reproduce as they do, continually in healthy human beings. The cell may lose its ability to reproduce, or it may reproduce incorrectly.

Cells that reproduce most frequently—such as those of the bone marrow, where blood cells are made—are hurt most by radiation. There is clear evidence that high radiation doses can cause **leukemia,** a malignant disease where the white blood cells multiply abnormally, and **cancer,** or dangerous growths in the body. Because reproducing cells are so sensitive, growing embryos and young children are especially susceptible to radiation damage.

Early researchers saw that large doses of radiation caused skin burns. They were unaware of damage caused by lower doses because it couldn't be seen or felt immediately. Consequently, radiation was used unsafely in science, medicine, and industry for many years.

Physicist Marie Curie won a Nobel Prize in physics in 1903 for the study of radiation, and in chemistry in 1911 for the discovery of radium and polonium. Her daughter, Irène Joliot-Curie, won a Nobel Prize in chemistry in 1935 for synthesis of new radioactive elements. Both of those great scientists died of leukemia.

Scientists can't perform experiments in which human beings are deliberately exposed to radiation to see what happens. All we know today comes from experiences of people who received massive doses from atomic bomb explosions, for medical reasons, or unintentionally in industry, and from laboratory experiments with animals.

Above: physicist and pioneer in
radiation research Marie Curie.
Right: the world's first nuclear explosion,
which took place on a testing range
in New Mexico in 1945.

Radiation sickness—effects such as nausea, vomiting, diarrhea, infection, and hemorrhage which can be deadly—is caused by a massive overdose of penetrating radiation from outside the body. **Radiation injury** consists of localized effects such as burns or loss of hair from overdoses of less penetrating external radiation.

Thousands of Japanese people received massive doses of radiation from the atomic bomb blasts of Hiroshima and Nagasaki in 1945. Several years afterward, survivors had significantly more cancers, leukemia, and eye cataracts than is normal.

Radiation poisoning is illness such as anemia or cancer that is caused by radiation from inside the body when dangerous amounts of radioactive materials are swallowed, breathed, or injected. A study was made of uranium miners in Czechoslovakia who breathed in radioactive radon gas (a daughter product found wherever uranium ore is) for many years. Those who worked in the mine at least ten years and lived at least ten years afterward died of lung cancer.

Until about a decade ago radiation from radium 226 was used to make watch dials glow in the dark. Women employed in the 1920s to paint these watch dials habitually made a point at the wet tips of their brushes by putting them (with radium) into their mouths. Many later suffered bone cancer and blood disorders as well as cancerous sores around the mouth.

GENETIC EFFECTS

Radiation can damage a person's genes, the tiny units that cause hereditary traits (like height, eye shade, and number of fingers) to be passed from parent to child. Then future descendants may be abnormal even if the parent seems perfectly well. The physical and mental well-being of future generations can be harmed by radiation since genes determine most aspects of living creatures.

Again, scientists don't know the exact way in which radiation damages human genes and reproductive organs. But there is a lot of convincing evidence that genetic damage does occur in all living things.

Biologist Herman J. Muller won a Nobel Prize in 1946 for finding hereditary effects of X rays on genes. His 1927 experiments with fruit flies showed that radiation can cause mutations (the sudden appearance of new characteristics which are not handed down from a parent). In addition, descendants of irradiated laboratory animals and children whose parents' reproductive organs were exposed to massive radiation doses have more genetic illnesses than normal populations.

Both father and mother contribute a gene for each trait inherited by their child. A gene mutation may be **dominant.** Then, it causes an observable result, such as extra fingers in a child who inherits the gene from just one parent. These effects appear in the first generation born after the mutation occurs.

The gene mutation may be **recessive.** Then it causes an observable result, such as sickle cell anemia, only if both parents contribute identical mutations. Such effects may not be seen for many generations or may never occur.

Mutations occur naturally. Children are not exact duplicates of their parents. Mutations apparently contribute to the evolution of species. Could a radiation-caused increase in the mutation rate be a good thing for humanity?

Scientists think that any increase in the mutation rate will be harmful to future generations. In every species they have studied, most mutations that have observable effects are harmful.

THRESHOLD OF SAFETY

Today we know that all ionizing radiation absorbed by the body can cause damage. Our bodies can repair some of the damage naturally with no apparent harm. Is there a precise safe amount we can absorb?

Threshold dose means the radiation dose required to cause cancer in the most susceptible (to radiation) person in the population. Below the threshold, cancer will not be induced by radiation. At or above it, cancer will be induced in susceptible individuals. The threshold dose idea is simple, but the question of whether or not a threshold dose actually exists is very controversial!

The effects of low levels of ionizing radiation on humans are not precisely known. Data come from high doses and high dose rates and animal experiments. Scientists disagree about how to use this data for predictions about low doses and low dose rates.

Are several low doses absorbed at different times as dangerous as a single equivalent large dose? No, if the body's natural mechanisms can repair some damage between times. Yes, if the damage is irreversible so that only the total amount of radiation accumulated matters.

[58]

Many radiation safety experts say that because of our incomplete knowledge we must assume that any amount of ionizing radiation, no matter how small, absorbed by a person involves some health risk for that person and/or future offspring.

Health physicist Karl Z. Morgan testified at 1978 Congressional hearings that, since much data show a statistically significant increase in cancer incidence following exposure to low doses of ionizing radiation, there can't be a threshold dose below which cancer risk is near zero.

The prestigious National Academy of Sciences issued a comprehensive report called "The Effects on Populations of Exposure to Low Levels of Ionizing Radiation" (the BEIR report) in 1972, in which all available data was evaluated. The BEIR report agrees that when making decisions about protecting people from radiation, we must assume there is no threshold below which the health risk is zero.

RADIATION UNITS

Three units are used to measure the effects of radiation.

The **roentgen** is a measure of the ionization produced in air by X and gamma rays.

The **rad** is a measure of the amount of ionizing radiation (any type) which is absorbed by any material.

The **rem,** acronym for **r**adiation **e**quivalent **m**an, is a measure of the biological effectiveness (or danger) of a given amount of radiation. For most practical purposes, these units can be used interchangeably, so 1 roentgen = 1 rad = 1 rem. A millirem means 1/1,000 of a rem.

SOURCES

Everyone in the world is exposed to radiation from natural sources. Cosmic radiation strikes from out in space. Terrestrial radiation comes from radioactive materials such as uranium and thorium inside the earth. The amount of natural radiation you receive depends on where you are.

Cosmic radiation is three times stronger at an altitude of 3,048 m (10,000 feet) than at sea level. It gets up to 20 percent stronger in going from the equator to 50° geomagnetic latitude. In the United States cosmic radiation doses range from about 38 millirem per year in Florida to 75 millirem per year in Wyoming. In the United Kingdom cosmic radiation doses are approximately 33 millirem per year.

Terrestrial radiation varies because there are different deposits of radioactive materials present at different spots on Earth. Gamma ray dose rates range from 15 to 35 millirem per year for the Atlantic and Gulf Coastal Plains to 75 to 140 millirem for the Colorado Plateau.

The BEIR report estimates that the total yearly average whole-body dose from natural radiation in the United States is at least 0.1 rem per year or some 7 rems in an average lifetime.

The amount of nonnatural radiation you are exposed to depends on how you live. At least 90 percent of radiation exposure from man-made sources in the United States is from medical and dental X rays. The rest comes from sources such as nuclear weapons testing and nuclear power production and consumer products such as radios, luminous dial watches and color TV sets.

We can't escape natural radiation entirely, but

we frequently have a choice about man-made radiation. These choices involve complex technical, economic, and social considerations. Radiation brings benefits accompanied by health risks. The dilemmas occur when we see no alternative way of obtaining those benefits we demand.

CHOICES

Public and personal choices involving the production and use of radiation confront us all. Some devices, such as medical and dental diagnostic instruments, produce radiation intentionally. Others, such as nuclear reactors in power plants, do so unintentionally.

Expected benefits tempt us. Increased health risks of the resulting radiation exposure concern us.

RADIATION DOSE LIMITS

Public policy today recognizes that the general public will be exposed to some man-made radiation. But the public must be safeguarded against radiation harm. Federal standards are set so we will not be exposed to an excessive amount of man-made (nonmedical) radiation.

Standards are continually reviewed as new facts are discovered. They have become increasingly strict since they were first set in 1929.

Currently, the Radiation Protection Guides set the maximum permissible dose for each of us from all man-made sources of radiation (except medical) at 170 millirem per year. There is no limit on radiation from medical practice.

Recognized national and international scientific bodies estimated that society could bear increased radiation risks from exposure limited to 170 millirems above natural radiation for expected benefits. Not all scientists agree. Some argue that the amount of man-made radiation to which people are exposed should be further reduced. Arthur R. Tamplin, a scientist with the U.S. Natural Resources Defense Council, said in 1978 Congressional hearings that estimates made only five years ago of the biological effects of radiation (both for cancer induction and genetic effects), are ten times too low.

Certain workers, such as medical radiation and nuclear reactor personnel, are exposed on the job to more ionizing radiation than usual. In the United States, the National Council on Radiation Protection and Measurements sets a maximum permissible radiation dose to protect them. **Maximum permissible dose** means that amount of radiation which, if received over a 50-year working time, likely won't produce observable radiation injury. Workers with radiation-connected jobs are not permitted by law to exceed a dose of 5 rems per year; 5 rems is also the maximum dose for workers in the United Kingdom with radiation-connected jobs.

The U.S. Environmental Protection Agency issued a proposal in 1978 entitled "Guidance for Occupational Radiation Exposure" which would lower existing (1969) radiation job exposure limits for workers at federal facilities and nuclear plants. The public participates in the creation of these rules.

MEDICAL AND DENTAL USES

The prescription of X rays by doctors and dentists is not regulated by law. Persons speaking for medical professional organizations argue that doctors' judgments are best, as they are for drugs. Other people want the law to regulate maximum levels of patient X-ray exposure.

Some scientists figure there are many patient deaths from leukemia due to irradiation. A large number of radiation scientists declare that the benefits of X-ray examination are much greater than any health risk. The BEIR report recommends reducing medical radiation exposure considerably and points out two ways to do so.

First, limit medical radiation exposure to clinically indicated procedures. For example, community-wide chest X rays should not be taken routinely. They are justified only when there is a good chance of significant detection of tuberculosis or pulmonary or heart disease.

Second, use efficient exposure techniques and radiation equipment under top operating conditions. A patient's reproductive organs should be covered by a protective shield to reduce the radiation that hits them whenever they are in or near the primary

X-ray beam unless shielding prevents accurate diagnosis. This shielding is especially important for all children and both males and females of child-bearing age to protect the well-being of future generations.

Dental X rays give very low doses to the reproductive organs. Still the American Dental Association and other groups recommend that patients wear a protective drape to reduce those doses about 90 percent further. Children, pregnant patients, and men and women of childbearing age particularly should be protected each time they have a dental X-ray examination.

The International Commission of Radiation Protection noted the special sensitivity of the embryo and fetus to ionizing radiation. Any woman who is pregnant or thinks she might be pregnant should not have X-ray examinations of the abdomen and pelvis unless absolutely necessary.

Radiation equipment should be subject to inspection and licensing. All radiation personnel should be required to have appropriate training and certification.

Every effort should be made to reduce the radiation exposure of patients without losing the information and benefits radiation gives!

Scientists are working on alternative ways to get the same benefits. Biophysicists developed a system that uses ultrasound waves (beyond the range of human hearing) plus computer processing in place of X rays to "see" inside a patient's body. Ultrasound has been used successfully in diagnosing heart problems. It is especially useful for taking pictures of a fetus where X rays are so dangerous.

NUCLEAR POWER

Today some 70 nuclear power plants generate about 10 percent of all the electricity in the United States. In the United Kingdom nine nuclear power stations generate 12.8 percent of electricity. Electricity is produced at power plants by spinning the shaft of a big electric generator. Steam is commonly used to make the shaft spin.

Steam is produced from water boiled by heat released from burning coal, oil, or gas (fossil fuels) in ordinary power plants. Nuclear power means the heat is released by splitting (fission) uranium 235 nuclei in a nuclear reactor. Except for the way heat is released, nuclear power production can be the same as ordinary power production.

Much less uranium 235 than fossil fuels is needed to generate a given amount of electricity. The **breeder reactor** even makes more new nuclear fuel ("breeds") as it operates. Nuclear power is affordable. It does not pollute the air with smoke. Nuclear fuel is available while the world's supply of fossil fuels is shrinking. Why then do protestors stage big public demonstrations, as they have in New Hampshire and California, to stop construction of controversial nuclear power plants?

All power plants may hurt us environmentally, but nuclear plants have a unique problem—radiation.

A nuclear fission reactor releases energy by converting uranium or plutonium fuel to lighter elements, some of which are radioactive. Some fission products become stable quickly, but others have long half-lives. Strontium 90 (28 years), cesium 137 (30 years), and krypton 85 (11 years) emit radiation for decades. Neutron bombardment also produces elements heavier than uranium. The most useful and dangerous of these is plutonium 239 whose half-life is 24,000 years.

People and the environment must be protected from radiation damage which could happen in several possible ways. Shielding must be provided that protects plant personnel and neighboring communities. Safeguards must prevent a major accident that would release enormously dangerous radiation and cause thousands of deaths. An American Physical Society study, recently questioned by government nuclear energy experts, found such safeguards presently acceptable but recommended a greatly expanded scheme of reactor safety research. The physicists indicated that it is not impossible for a major accident to occur but that it is much less likely than other industrial risks that society accepts.

There is no completely satisfactory method of permanently disposing of the long-lived radioactive wastes so far. They are mostly stored in steel tanks now. Plutonium causes the most worry, then cesium 137 and strontium 90. The U.S. Department of Energy is looking for ways the federal government might store spent nuclear reactor fuel. Research on burying radioactive wastes in salt mines or in the ocean floor continues.

Plutonium can be recovered from spent fuel and used as new fuel. But there are associated risks. Alpha rays from plutonium, the most hazardous element known, are deadly if even a tiny bit of the element enters the body. Also, only a few kilograms of plutonium are needed to make a deadly atomic bomb.

Harvard student Dimitri Rotow designed seemingly workable nuclear bombs by himself in 1978 using public information after only a year of college-level physics. The possibility of plutonium bombs home-made by terrorists threatens the world. Nuclear facilities and materials must be carefully monitored at all times to protect society from dreadful misuses of radioactive materials.

The Nuclear Regulatory Commission (NRC) is responsible for regulating nuclear power in the United States. It has some of the most difficult engineering and political dilemmas of this century. Supporters of nuclear power say NRC plant regulations are too strict. Critics say the NRC is too lax in the area of safety and health. NRC decisions affect us all.

Estimates by the Nuclear Regulatory Commission in 1975 claim that the odds for an accident in a motor vehicle were 1 in 4,000 and for a nuclear reactor accident, 1 in 5,000,000,000.

NUCLEAR WARFARE

Human beings have over 50,000 nuclear bombs ready to blast their world to bits. If used, these would release horrendous amounts of radioactivity. Just one could kill and badly injure millions of people and make a large area unfit for human life. Yet production of nuclear weapons continues.

Nations developing nuclear weapons want to make sure they will explode as intended. Tests release ionizing radiation into the environment immediately and the products strontium 90, cesium 137, cobalt 60, and plutonium stay menacing for years.

In 1946, the United States chose Bikini, a coral atoll in the Marshall Islands of the Pacific Ocean, as a nuclear weapons test site. Bikinians were moved to Kili Island, 800 km (500 miles) away. Examinations in 1977 showed the groundwater and vegetation on Bikini to be still dangerously radioactive. Over 100 Bikinians who had returned when the atoll was presumed safe showed a startling increase of radioisotopes in their bodies. They had to move again. The U.S. Department of Energy scheduled an aerial radiation survey of the Marshall Islands for the end of 1978 to find out precisely what radiation hazard remains from nuclear testing there during the 1940s and 1950s.

Between 1946 and 1964 the United States exploded over 180 nuclear weapons in the atmosphere. An estimated 500,000 soldiers were ordered into the test site during or right after many of these blasts. They apparently have developed more cancers than normal, although they supposedly got only low doses of ionizing radiation previously thought safe.

When tests are done in the atmosphere, moving air masses carry radioactive debris around the world. Radioisotopes from a 1977 Chinese nuclear explosion in the atmosphere arrived over the United States within a week. Rain can bring the radioisotopes (fallout) to earth, contaminating sources of food and drinking water.

The United States hasn't tested nuclear weapons in the atmosphere since 1963. At that time it joined the USSR and other nations in signing a treaty which bans such above-ground tests. Worldwide fallout today is due to long-lived radioisotopes released before 1963 plus debris from subsequent tests by nonsigners.

The newest nuclear terror is the neutron bomb.

It is supposed to kill and destroy on target but not damage buildings and equipment a few hundred yards away. People on the fringe of the battle may suffer horrible lengthy radiation injuries but their property will not be hurt.

Atomic bombs and hydrogen bombs are built to destroy everything by their blast and heat. Neutron bombs have a lower yield, or explosive force, and kill mainly by their energetic gamma rays and neutrons.

A neutron bomb whose deadly radiation would kill everyone within a mile of the target wouldn't destroy things 500 m (550 yards) from it. A conventional nuclear bomb big enough to spread deadly radiation that far would spread blast and fire over 20 km (12 miles) from the target.

Nuclear-powered robot spies "watch" the nuclear arms race with radiation-sensitive "eyes" as they orbit Earth. Cosmos 954 was one such Soviet spacecraft that watched American ship positions. Its fiery descent to Earth in 1978, in Canada, reminded the world of further radiation threats. Cosmos 954 was powered by a nuclear reactor fueled by 45 kg (100 pounds) of uranium 235.

CONSUMER PRODUCTS

Experts recently looked at available scientific data on radiation sources encountered in daily life, for the National Council on Radiation Protection and Measurements (NCRP). Their 1977 report is entitled "Radiation Exposure from Consumer Products and Miscellaneous Sources." It gives facts and figures to help people weigh the health risks against benefits of a variety of goods.

Some things aren't worth the amount of radiation exposure they cause. Radium 226 should not be used as the activating agent to make watches and clocks glow in the dark. Tritium or promethium, both radioactive, can be used instead. Their content (unlike radium) is limited in timepieces according to federal safety regulations.

X-ray fluoroscopes should not be used to see if shoes fit, as they commonly were 25 years ago. Often they are banned by law.

Sometimes jobs can be done equally well by different means that don't involve radiation exposure at all. Personnel inspection, done by X-ray scanning units for security purposes in World War II and in prisons, is an example.

Other jobs seem worthwhile, but no better way is known. Here the goal should be to keep radiation exposure at a minimum. Airport baggage X-ray inspection devices and smoke detectors that contain alpha ray emitters (americium 241 or radium 226) are regulated to minimize radiation hazards.

Smoke detectors are commonly used in public and commercial buildings as well as in homes. Manufacturers must label units with information on proper, safe disposal. The NCRP expects more and more smoke detectors to be used in homes and proposes to re-evaluate their safety periodically.

Color TV sets emit unwanted X rays when operating. Since 1970, U.S. federal law requires color TV sets to perform so that viewers sitting several feet back from the screen receive practically no radiation exposure. New sets are monitored by manufacturers and government authorities. They are checked in plants and government laboratories. It seems reasonably safe to watch color TV programs if you don't sit too close to the set.

Products that people have long been accustomed to enjoying may involve significant natural radiation exposures but seem to be beyond government control. Tobacco contains lead 210 and polonium 210 which may increase radiation doses to the lungs of cigarette smokers. Uranium, thorium, or potassium in brick, granite, and concrete buildings give more radiation than adjacent wooden structures. Uranium and thorium in highway granites or phosphates have higher than nearby off-highway radiation levels.

The NCRP report estimates that the average radiation dose in the United States from consumer products totals less than 5 millirem per year.

SPACE FRONTIERS

Space promises new places to settle, material resources, and exciting explorations. But space is full of deadly ionizing radiation. There are X rays, gamma rays, and energetic electrons, protons, neutrons, and alpha particles.

Cosmic rays from our galaxy are always a source of highly penetrating ionizing radiation. Galactic cosmic rays shoot about 10 rems a year into anything not shielded.

Gigantic solar flares (violent eruptions on the sun that pour high energy protons into space) can deliver many tens of rems. Once a flare has begun, energetic particles strike out for a day or more in all directions. People not in a shielded place would have little time to get to one.

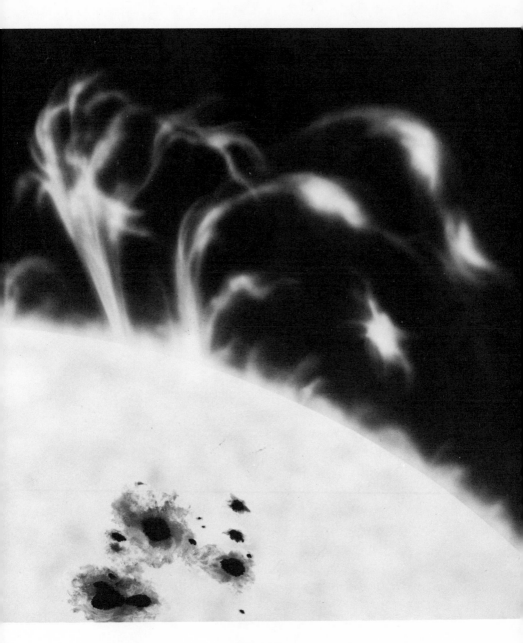

A solar flare.

On Earth we are protected from space radiation by our atmosphere and the force of Earth's magnetic field. Air is an effective shield against deadly high-energy electromagnetic waves and particles.

Air gets ten times thinner for each 16 km (10 miles) of altitude. At about 100 km (60 miles), air density is only one millionth that at sea level.

There is no air in space. But protecting humans from space radiation is an engineering problem that we hope to solve. Astronauts have been successfully shielded from radiation in spacecraft orbiting Earth and in spacesuits on our airless moon.

By the time human beings explore Mars, settle in colonies in space, or fly starships to distant unknown worlds in the twenty-first century, they should be shielded from space radiation as safely as we are on Earth.

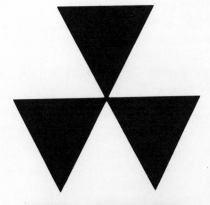

SELECTED BIBLIOGRAPHY

So much material has been and is being published on radiation that only selected references are listed below.

TECHNICAL PUBLICATIONS

The Effects on Populations of Exposure to Low Levels of Ionizing Radiation. Washington: National Academy of Sciences, National Research Council, 1972.

Evolution of Occupational Hazards from Industrial Radiation: A Survey of Selected States. Cincinnati: U.S. Department of Health, Education, and Welfare, National Institute for Occupational Safety and Health, 1976.

Radiation Exposure from Consumer Products and Miscellaneous Sources, NCRP Report no. 56. Washington: National Council on Radiation Protection and Measurements, 1977.

Report to the American Physical Society by the Study Group on Light-Water Reactor Safety, published as Supplement no. 1 to volume 47 of the *Reviews of Modern Physics.* New York: American Physical Society, 1975.

TECHNICAL REFERENCES

American Institute of Physics Handbook, 3d. ed. Dwight E. Gray, coordinating editor. New York: McGraw-Hill Book Co.

Van Nostrand's Scientific Encyclopedia, 5th ed. New York: Van Nostrand Reinhold Co.

POPULAR BOOKS AND PUBLICATIONS

Brannigan, Francis L. *Living With Radiation.* Washington: U.S. Department of Energy, formerly USERDA, 1976.

Cohen, Bernard L. *Nuclear Science and Society.* New York: Anchor Press/Doubleday, 1974.

Kastner, Jacob. *Nature's Invisible Rays.* Washington: U.S. Department of Energy, formerly USERDA, 1973.

Laws, Priscilla. *X-Rays: More Harm Than Good?* Emmaus, PA: Rodale Press, 1977.

Marion, Jerry B. *Essential Physics in the World Around Us.* New York: John Wiley & Sons, 1977.

Moché, Dinah. *Astronomy,* Wiley Self-Teaching Guides. New York: John Wiley & Sons, 1978.

Moché, Dinah. *Search for Life Beyond Earth.* New York: Franklin Watts, 1978.

Schroeer, Dietrich. *Physics and Its Fifth Dimension Society.* Reading, MA: Addison-Wesley Publishing Co., 1972.

Spruch, Grace Marmor and Larry Spruch. *The Ubiquitous Atom.* New York: Charles Scribner's Sons, 1974.

INDEX

Fractures, 31
Friedman, Herbert, 38

Gadolinium **153,** 35
Gamma rays, 5, 6–7, 8, 9, 12,
    13, 30, 38, 39, 43, 47, 48, 58
    to make pictures, 34–35
    used for sterilization, 49–
        50, 57, 64
Gastrointestinal x-rays, 32
Gauges, radiation, 46, 47
Geiger counters, 9
Gene mutations, 57
Generators, radioisotope
    thermoelectric, 51
Genetic effects, of radiation,
    56–58, 63
Geology, 25–28, 29
Giacconi, Riccardo, 38
Gravity, 38

Half-life
    of carbon **14,** 23
    of radioisotopes, 8, 9, 22,
        23, 25, 40
Heart disease, 32, 64, 65
Health problems, radioiso-
    topes used to diagnose, 13–
    18, 31–33, 63, 64–65
Heat, as electromagnetic ra-
    diation, 4, 5
Helium, 6
Heredity. **See** Genetic effects
High energy astronomy, 35–38
Highjacking, 34, 71
Hiroshima, 56
Hormones, 44, 45
Humans, effect of radiation on,
    5–6, 9, 13, 18, 44–45, 52–61,
    63, 67, 68–70, 71

Hydrogen, 6, 7
    bomb, 70

Industry, 12, 20
    radiation used to control,
        46–48, 49
Infrared radiation, 4
Insect sprays, 18
International Commission of
    Radiation Protection, 65
Iodine **131,** 13
Ionizing radiation, 9. **See also**
    Radiation
Ions, 8–9
Iron **59,** 20
Irradiation, 48–50, 57, 64
Isotopes, 7, 23, 25. **See also**
    Radioisotopes

Joliot-Curie, Irène, 53
Jupiter, 51

Krypton, 13, 47, 66

Law enforcement, neutron ac-
    tivation analysis used for,
    40–41, 45
Lead **206,** 25
Lead, used in paint, 41, 43
Leukemia, 53, 56, 64
Light, as electromagnetic radi-
    ation, 4, 5
Lixiscope, 33
Lung disease, 13–18, 64

Madsen, James H. Jr., 25
Mars, signs of life on, 19–20,
    74
Materials, affect of radiation
    on, 8–9

ABOUT THE
AUTHOR

Dinah L. Moché is the author of seven books for young readers, including **Search for Life Beyond Earth** and **Mars** for Franklin Watts.

An Associate Professor of Physics and Astronomy at Queensborough Community College of CUNY, Dr. Moché has received many professional awards and research grants. In 1976 she was awarded a National Science Foundation Faculty Fellowship in Science.

Dr. Moché received her B.A. degree from Harvard-Radcliffe College, and her M.A. and Ph.D. from Columbia University. She lives with her family in Mamaroneck, N.Y.